Saudade - A Collection of Poetry
by Donovan James

Saudade - sow-DAH-dj- Adjective -
A deep emotional state of nostalgic or deeply melancholic
longing for an absent something or someone that one
loves. It often carries a repressed knowledge that the
object of longing will never return.

2013 Curious Apes Publishing—First Paperback Edition
www.curiousapespublishing.com

Cover Art by Andrea Rae
www.languageisalie.com

Published in The United States of America
ISBN: 978-0-9910088-2-7

Thank you
for reading.

Part 1:

Part 2:

Part 1

Annabel Lee's Tavern

I awoke to you laying next to me,
But it was all a dream.
You were naked and bare,
Geometric perfection in your hourglass curves,
And your hair smelled of a kiwi breeze.
You awoke and we danced underneath the sheets,
Before rising to dine at the place you love,
And I remember the feel of the warm spring air,
And I clasped your hand as we walked there.

I awoke to you laying next to me,
But it was all a dream.
I cannot comprehend why you cannot reconcile,
Your wants and your memes,
Are your intangible beliefs worth more,
Than the tangible time we share?
The happiness of this life sacrificed,
For the potential of a fulfilled promise,
Of the afterlife.
Or is my lack of faith frightening to you?
An alien undercurrent of cold unabiding logic.

I awoke, not to you, but to no one,
Alone again amongst the sheets,
I danced with myself out of necessity,
Then rose and walked through the chill spring air,
To the place you love, and waited for you there.

Old Friends

It's hard to tell when old friends have changed,
Assumptions and memories
Cloud our perceptions,
Leaving candor adrift
In a debris field,
And hiding the contradictions,
Of who we believe,
The other to be.

Standing in
The middle of a river,

Time

I can see forms taking shape:
You, inevitably married,
Watching for the pratfalls
That captured your father,
And battling Man's need
To make,
"Something"
Of his life,
But the greatest legacies are nothing but stories,
Amongst apes,
And the most magnificent buildings nothing,
But dust,
In a different time.

The other half,
Your old friend,
Has been alone for so long,
Surely something has broken,
Perhaps, the ability to trust,
Or worse,
The desire,
And surely something has grown,
Perhaps, his lofty expectations,
A philosophy stemming from
His, yours, our
Broken homes,
"Do you think yours will last?"
He asks,
Silence gives a telling reply.

I can see a future forming,
Where you visit this recluse,
Telling your wife,
"It's what you do."
He's still pounding away on those keys,
Believing in the salvation of words,
But never their recognition,
He is insistent,
That all will be forgotten.

"Why continue, then?"
You tentatively ask him,
And his whiskey replies:
"Hope is a feeble candle,
Fueled by belief, by a will.

But what sustains such a
Feeble thing?"
You reply,
"The will is you, man."

"I know,"
He says,
"That is why I must write,
For I can feel the darkness encroaching,
And the will,
Extinguishing.
And what will remain
When it's gone?"

The night becomes enveloped by,
Empty beer bottles that spur lost jokes,
Cashed bowls that dust off
Old trust,
And allow a vulnerability
To seep into our words,
Until,
They become confessions:

"Do you remember when?"
"Of course I do man…"
We laugh at our old sincerity,
Our hope and naivety,
Now firmly clasped behind
The lessons of becoming men,
And the realism required
To survive the modern world,

They leave no time for meaning,
Or money in caring,
Which is why even those moments
Of heartbreak and betrayal,
words
now
so
watered
down
Are meaningful in our mental records.

We had not yet allowed,
Cynicism
To become our default opinion.

But still,
The stories of youth gain glory
From old men reminiscing.
And,
"Do you remember when…?"
"Of course I do man…"
Resonates
In the melody of a lost loved one.

Morning comes and the airport beckons,
Coffee is guzzled
To dim the dull grin of a hangover,
To no avail.

We are men saying goodbye in a crowd,
What tears will be shed?
None.
They are outside the spectrum of
Masculinity,
Whatever honest words wish to slip thru,
Are censored.

We are both already
Lost
Again in the river.

You watch the tarmac fall,
Grateful for silence's
Lack of requirements.
You finally get to feel nothing,
Until,
The plane descends,
And a life greets you,
One you can never truly combine,
With your youth,
Nor should you try.

He watches the plane ascend,
Until,
It disappears.
Leaving the sudden clarity of
A solitary life,

And the companion of
Nihilism,
To greet him,
Again
He pours a glass of whiskey,
And sits down.
Surely,
He should be able to write
Something.

Perhaps…

Goodbye,
Old friend,
Until I have the pleasure,
Of reminiscing
With you again.

One Night Stands

Apparently, it's morning.
Stubborn sunlight won't let me sleep,
Vague recollections putter in from the previous night,
But I really just want her to leave.

What did I say that led you to bed?
A passionate artist's serenade
Sung over endless pints?
Or the stoic strength of a mysterious outsider?
Or, my newest incarnation:
The humbled man hoping to create a home.

Vomit bubbles up in my mouth,
I swallow it.
Rookie mistakes on repeat:
For her place is always better suited for an escape,
She rolls over—I pretend to sleep,
Sigh,
Still she does not leave.

I always used them only for sex,
But now I am lonely,
And use them as transient companions,
How sad,
Stealing intimacy from strange women.

I hate the whole process—
(what it admits about my own weakness)
—And the ease at which they submit.
Surely this is a sign I'm growing older,
Perhaps the humbled man is not a ploy at all.

Casa, 2007, Cabernet Sauvignon

I started drinking alone,
Around eight,
Laughed alone with the lights
Along the walls,
Accompanied by wavelengths,
And the diaries of authors encased in dank frames,
While friends simmer
With soon to be wives,
Others marry their careers,
These unions allied against death.
Everyone's life,
Perfectly in chord
To the standard plan.

I open a bottle of wine,
One I was saving for a special occasion,
But a forgettable,
Easily misplaced,
Night of a young man's life,
Will suffice.

Death arrives,
Fleeting in and out,
(I can only understand him
For small moments of time),
But the wine provides courage,
Abiding the fear,
And I consider him.

I will be this ill equipped ape
When I face him,
The final time,
When it's not flirtatious
But an appointment instead.
Will I be burnt,
Used up,
And ready?
Or will I hold regrets,
Each one a mental burden,
Marking clearly,
Failures of the most permanent,
Unforgivable and unchangeable,
The unrelievable weight of finality.

I awake,
Sort of,
Consciousness loads slowly,
But the hangover hits immediately.
I get up,
Arm outward as I let
A long stream of piss
Fill the toilet.
The bottle of wine is empty
And whatever wisdom it gave me,
Gone.

Why can we only hold,
One parcel of wisdom,
In our heads at a time?
If only we could grasp
Multiple truths at once,
At all moments,
What failures we could erase,
What decisions we could cull,

What gods we could be.

Great Apes, Great Mistakes

There once was an ape,
With the ability to think.
He had many nights alone to himself,
In which to ask a perplexing question:
Why?
There was no answer, of course,
His death,
--Which always remained
Of the utmost importance to himself,
Was irrelevant to the rest of existence.

Ponder this,
Dammit,
Ponder this,
For I have your time now.
Your death,
—Which always remains
Of the utmost importance to you,
Is irrelevant to the rest of existence.

You see,
This ape had learned too much.
He no longer had the room
In his brain,
For the flawed but false lies,
Of meaning and religion,
The poor bastard.

But the most marvelous of all
His advancements,
Was that he could hold,
Two realities in his mind;
A lie and the truth,
And remember them both.
This was how he used,
That massive brain,
And of course,
To deem himself
Separate from the planet,
And greater than the other animals,
Whom he tortured and raped.

To ameliorate these,
Difficult and unsettling truths,
He imbibed a bounty of alcohols,
And one day met a girl,
With whom he had a child,
And when the child asked,
"What happens when you die?"
The man told his father's lie,
The one that birthed those nights into existence,

For he assumed the child stupider than he,
And would struggle under the stark truth,
And thus each successive generation
Was borne underneath this burden,
To come to terms with two realities:
That life has meaning,
And that it does not.

A malady easily remedied:
There's no need,
To lie to the children at all.

A Woman Worthy Of Being Loved

Some days I am bursting with love,
And I daydream who the recipient of
It will be. Surely a sign of loneliness,
But I ignore this:
I daydream of many things and none of them
Define me to such a permanent,
Self-pitying emotion.

I day dream of the ways I would love a woman
Worthy of being loved,
And then I wonder,
If my standards are too high,
Sentencing me to solitude,
As opposed to a suitable companion,
Tenure achieved through pure perfunctory,
She would not challenge me,
Incite or anger me,
Nor inspire me.
A lazy relationship resting on abandoned shores
Of love and hope and dreams,
Of the way I'd love my love to be.

I am not afraid of dying alone,
Afraid of death, yes,
No one escapes the fear nor the fate,
And so,
I wait,
For a woman worthy of being loved,

And if she never comes,
My empathetic heart,
Who's bleeding summons these words,
Will plump, engorge and enlarge,
It will bounce against the walls of my chest,
Like an atom too energetic to be compressed,
Wishing for a woman,
Any woman,
For relief,
So that these
Ideas of romantic getaways,
And impromptu surprises,
Of random eskimo kisses,
And hard day massages,
Escape.

But I tell it to wait.
And if it suffocates,
So be it.

I will not fake it.

Pissing In The Dark

The key to my heart, my head,
My friendship, my trust,
My soul, my love,
Is in these words
I pluck from smoky thoughts.

They serve as expression;
I am the type of person,
That must announce his opinions,
And emotions,
My nudeness must stand in stark contrast,
To all the liars sentiments of strength,
Too timid to admit
That they too feel things
Unsanctioned by social pressures,
And someday they may succeed,
Burying emotions so deep,
That they appear
To have never bloomed.

My words serve as an explorer
Into realms I cannot physically travel,
A thousand arms grasping,
In the dark,
For that spark of connection between two humans,
In words and touch and time,
Lives, for a moment, intertwined.

I toss these words
Like balloons with strings too short to grasp,
Or notes encased in glass,
Wandering upon a tussled shore,
And I hope they return with people who like them,
A brother, companion,
Or lover,
Who feel the things I've felt,
So that I can say:

You are not alone, friend,
Nor am I,
Anymore.

Darling, jump!

It's "just" out of a plane and I swear it's safe,
Afterwards we can dine in a dive bar and down PBRs,
Get busted for public sex and skip on the bill,
And roam the sandy streets bumming strangers for weed.

Darling, Congrats!
You've graduated under a stormy sky,
But we celebrate too hard,
(Sorry),
And you're sick, across the sheets,
I'll do the same in due time,
And I showed you Coronado, the sun setting
Into the Pacific,
What if we returned here,
In years,
And I proposed?
Would your heart have melted straight into the sea?
Regardless, the idea,
Occurred to me…

Darling, giggle!
When I come up, and reach for the sheets
To wipe my mouth clean,
We'll become intimate, and in contrast,
I'll lay limply on top of you,
- a joke -
The giggles erupt
Into uncontrollable laughter,

These are the things I remember.

Darling, goodbye!
I love you too much to lead you on,
It's an engagement, my even being around,
Your wild days are gone and mine have just begun,
You're ready to settle down, foreign streets call my name,
And in a daydream I can see your hand,
In the center of a crowd of single girls,
Who's ooh's and ahh's inflate your elated smile,
And that smile is the last thing I see,
I concede the dream to another suitor.

Fuckers.

I work with this fucker,
She's all bleached blonde
And sinewy flesh,
The lines of her face
Only coalesce,
Where frowns and scowls and screams
Require strength.

This fucking day,
Was an early morning shift,
Where she was closing
Of course,
So I was there till six,
Giving me only enough time
For a quick bite, a few beers,
I was scheduled to read
A poem, a political rag
That skewered Americans,
At eight.

I walked to my car,
Where glass littered the lot,
In tiny, individual cubes,
Like humans,
After the emotions manifesting a mob have fled.
They ambled without purpose,
Resting in the seat as evidence,
That my duffel bag full of clothes
Was gone,
The laptop too.

Those words, poems, stories

Gone.

The fucker didn't have the hands,
To take the guitar,
Too.

I drink,
Heavily and quickly,
Immediately its eight,
And I read the words violently,
An insane interrogator, eviscerating
His own words,
Wondering, how
Can any of us say no to our desires?
I drink I drink I drink.

"Why is he so angry?"
You fuckers don't know what I lost,
You still write your words,
In books,
By hand,
To *look* like a writer.
I
lost
pieces
I can never replace.

I drink and began talking
To a brunette at the bar,
For an hour or so, until,
"Hey, we should get drinks.
Somewhere else."
The fucker replies,
"I have a boyfriend."

Of course she waited
Till I'd bought her a few drinks,
To tell me this,
Because,
To her,
What I have lost?
Nothing.
Who am I?
No one.

I stumble back to the hostel,
Where a vagabond of forty,
Lean and angry,
And a Norwegian blonde
Invite me to an underground bar,
To play poker,
But the vagabond gets lost,
Of course,
And by the time we get there the game
Is over,
And we can't even get a drink.

I tell an old friend,
He says,
"That's like me losing a family member."
I say,
"Am I that alone,
You fucker?"

I tell a girl,
And she says,
"What compels someone to do that?"
The world, darling,
The world.

I get to work,
And the blonde fucker says,
"Snap out of it,
I ain't payin'
You to stand around."

I don't bother,
To tell that fucker,
What I've lost.
That'll just cause the rust
From her melodious,
Orgasmic muscles to disperse,
And then,
I'll see this fucker,
Happy.

Vows

I wrote a love song for you,
Even though I've never met you,
But maybe when I do,
Can we burn this paper together?

Wisk you away on a Friday night,
To a Paris hotel of hedonistic delights
I'll propose under a starlit night,
And make love to you forever.

We'll roll around in thousand threaded sheets,
I'll lose myself when you smile at me,
We'll get tipsy with French wine by the sea,
And I'll make love to you forever.

And I'll hold up this crumpled poem,
Tangible evidence of my loneliest time,
And we'll set it aflame as your lips touch mine,
And I'll make love to you forever.

"Letters To Amanda"

An old friend told me,
He was in love today.
The girl is blonde and young,
And by all outward appearances,
Happy.

He told me he loves her problems,
Her humor,
And other intangibles.
Like how she'll win in arguments,
Leaving him stunned, silent,
Irises slanted towards the ground,
Matching
A respectful frown,
"Goddamn,
She did it again…"

He hopes to succeed,
Where his parents failed.
Their oral histories old heirlooms
And he searches them for solutions,
Assuring himself,
He'll act differently.

But maybe it always ends the same,
The same fights transmuted through the years,
Tarnishing love we believe to be so
Unique.

I never told him,
I had an idea for a poem
To be titled:
"Letters To Amanda,"
For my friend sends her letters,
Physical letters you can hold
In the mail every day,
Of what he's thinking,
Of who he is that morning,
(For who knows who
We will be when we awake),
And he needs her to know,
Whoever he is,
Whatever issues he wrestles,
That he loves her.

And in this short, short life,
What is sweeter,
Than a young blonde girl
Receiving a letter,
Telling her,
She is loved?

Lust

You are never far from my thoughts.
I sit,
In a cube,
Thinking of you.

Great gifts are testaments
To how a person listened,
To your rants,
Rambles,
Whiskey spurring an avalanche of
Tumbling confessions,
Burying a confused cynicism,
It's all encompassing theory facing
An impenetrable exception.

What does it mean for someone to care,
To listen?
Or rather,
To take in our consciousness
In time evading talks,
And in their solace,
Transmute it into
Manifested affection.

I watch you opine,
Through eyes blurred
With infatuation, enlivening
The dingy shards of light
From this dive bar.

I don't actually hear anything you say.

I think…
I want to lick the sweat off your back,
Douse myself in your scent,
Pull your hair up and kiss
The nape of your neck.

I want to pleasure you,
Until my tongue has caressed
Every groove,
And taste you every time I breathe,
I want passion to produce a magnetic connection,
That draws my chest,
And cheek,
To yours,
I want to French kiss you while inside of you,
Move my hand from your back to your palm,
Encasing it,
The intimate tenderness turns me on.

I want to find the rhythm with you,
Hips spotting themselves across
This threaded dance floor,
Comfort encouraged by a smile,
A moan,
The flames of desire
Erase the filaments of inhibition,
And pleasure is spread across
The surging wavelengths of passion,

In the vast
boundless
land
Of making love.

....

It ends
With a long exhale,
Frozen
In the explosion of blindness,
Until
I collapse around you.

We awake.
And of course,
I still want more,

"Will you stay the night?"

Love

I wake thinking of you,
And carry these unrequited pines around,
Return to such a silent home,
Amongst appliances, chairs,
All emotionless,

I am a shadow in the middle of a desert.

I idly decide to amble
Through the cemetery,
For I have nothing better to do.
Accompanied by great ancestral trees,
I sift through graves
And think,

I could spend all my afternoons
Walking through parks with you,
And never worry of another
Misspent second.
I wonder,
If our kisses or thrusts,
Would be as seamless as these talks,
Or even if
You'd let me hold your hand,
Although, you shouldn't:

It is not innocent.

I enter the home
You share with her,
And speciously hide treason
Behind asinine praise.
If I kissed you,
Threw you down on this chaise lounge,
Would you let me
Detonate,
The life you've built,
With her?

We are the tightrope walkers,
Of this precarious rope of platonic love,
To ask for more,
To declare what my heart resonates for,
Would be to shove you off,
And watch you fall.

So....
I keep my feelings secret,
Refusing to burden you
With a choice I'll lose,
Me,
Or her?

But,
I thank you,
For dusting the rust off my old jalopy
Of a heart;
I didn't really think I was capable
Of feeling these
Things,

Through all this scar tissue,
This affection, this desire,
Love,
From the spiritual center of my being
To this physical realm,
My love for you lights this distance,
You are,
The creator of stars across
The universe of my consciousness.

It is getting dark;
I have circled the cemetery three times,
And finally stumble upon
the grave,
Of a twelve year old boy.
The stone says he,
"Loved chocolate,"
And hints upon some disability,
That surely discounted his years,
I ponder,
All the things he missed.

The flowers are still fresh.

Above A Raging Sea

Who am I when I only interact,
Never reflect?
A bulbous Id,
Knocking against
Materialistic walls,
Believing the echoes to be,
Clefs of a
Harmonious self.

We collect identities through
Blabbering talks:
Surely,
This is me.
After all,
I *am* speaking.

We are not our reflections upon others,
But the churning boil behind our eyes,
The N-th dimensional tubes,
Composed of
All experiences and the Id itself,
And of course,
The rambling spewing thoughts,
We pretend to control,
Or...
Will.

A securely constructed self
Stands,
Still against the ravaging winds
Of culture.
There is no time to think,
To reflect,
Only to act to speak to run,
Carnivorous company gobbles up time,
Fleeing from their own fears of
Loneliness,
Unaware of the divine
Vitamin of being alone.

We blindly burn friends
In the ways we hate being burned,
Justified outrage bellows,
"Can you believe
They didn't even invite *us*?"
Nor we them,
But our misforgivings elope
As promises in the wind.

Who do we become,
When we only
Do
Never
Be?

Elongated selves surfing through
Our lives,
Consequences as mysterious
As the lives behind our eyes.

Who do we become,
When we only
Do
Never
Be?

Till Death Do Us Part

When we're old and grey, baby,
And our courtship days are faded memories,
Like yellow framed photographs
Atop the dusty shelves of our loony minds,

And our youth's relinquished,
Replaced by droopy wrinkles
And me, I've got my spotted bald head,
And you, your muffin top bun of grey hair,

And when we eat our meals of mush,
In contented routine silence,
Popping pills to achieve our old people perfume,
I ponder, if you still swoon from my smile,
A rusty heart skipping a stingy beat.

Happiness

I apologize for this:
A topic too suited
For sentimentality,
And its sister, banality,
Still, here it goes:

My thoughts careen off the cliff of happiness,
And only when they realize this,
Do they begin to fall.
For it is always only a moment,
A fleeting state of being,
The Schrödinger's test of
Psychoanalysis.

Gone,
My symptoms of shame,
An overall malaise,
More so then a tangible wart.

Gone,
My time traveling machines of regret,
Transporting me to a mixtape
Of my greatest mistakes.

Gone,
My responsibilities to my family,
To credit card debtors,
To student loan collectors,

And, of course,
To paycheck presenters.

Gone,
The denial of death,
Instead, an insane acceptance,
The delusion I understand its consequence.

Gone,
The loneliness of being alone,
In its place, a strength that only comes,
From settling into one's own atoms.

It is the things I do not feel.
An unhampered man roaming free
In the prairies of consciousness,
Then,
The moment passes,
And again,
I am mired in the miseries of men.

Crime

Do I think it's a crime?
That I think about you from time to time?
That wistful thoughts of you and I,
Idle through my mind?

The Suchness And The Void

Is anxiety a measure of regret?
Or of things unaddressed?
We live adrift
In ape avatars sharing reality,
Blurting out utterances from meat holes,
That are somehow supposed to convey
Enlightenment,
Consciousness, the Suchness and the Void,
Of all the things that exist behind our eyes,
That we call "me."

Spirituality is the spectrum of reality,
That exists behind every conscious creature.
Long tentacles extending behind our eyes,
Constituted of the mess we call
Consciousness,
Memories,
Insecurities and hopes,
The inexpressible Suchness and the Void.
Long invisible tentacles tinted,
In colors outside our observable world,

Our lovers are not
Tranquil thighs,
Or symmetric smiles signaling
Potential ape mates,
But these tentacles composed of emotions,
Future reactions, of mistakes and wisdom.

Is anxiety a measure of regret?
Or a word we give to panic,
Sneaking out
From accepting "realistic expectations,"
Repressing failures to a low resonance,
That's never quite,
Silent enough,
For what our lives
Have become.

Or is anxiety the symptom of sorrow
Seeping up from silent fates,
Their tentacles composed of
Our inaction, the CEO's greed, their suffering,
Their ape bodies thrashing against
Loss,
Grasping for a humane branch of survival,
Held,
Out of reach,
At the profit line's leisure.

Suffering is a segment of
Our shared reality,
It's symptoms bleed into our tentacles,
Churning nebulous voices into a moshing mob,
As we try,
Desperately
To drown spiritualistic diseases
With materialistic fetishes,
And when all that fails,

We tell ourselves
That this is just how,
It has,
To be:

"The world is a circus!
A horrifying madhouse!
Where it's perfectly sane,
To devote most resources
Towards annihilating fellow apes."

So perhaps,
Anxiety is a measure of defeat.
The loss of those ideals you once believed,
The ghost of love chained
To the machine for eternity.
While the gargantuan arm of civilization
Crushes life and life and life.

But they'll crawl up on quiet nights,
Swarming over your consciousness,
Whispering
What you've always known:

That it simply
Does not
Have to be,
This way.

Interlude

Dialogue with God

"Please sir, may I have more time?"

"What do you need more time for?"

"Things, sir, I didn't get to buy everything it was that I wanted!"

"What do you want?"

"So much, dear sir! A boat, a car, a mansion!"

"Why?"

"Because I need them, dear sir! They're important to me!"

"Objects of importance are those that we care for, old man. What use are these *things* to you now?"

"Oh, I see your point, dear sir. In that case, may I have more time?"

"What do you need more time for?"

"For money, sir! I don't need the things, I need the *money* to buy more *things*!"

"But money is nothing but time in a different form. And did I not give you time for as much money as you could acquire?"

"Well, yes, but it simply wasn't enough."

"I find that hard to believe. You had 80 years. That's more than most are lucky enough to receive."

"But what is a year? It changes as time goes on!"

"What do you mean?"

"Well, at first, it—"

"What do you mean at first?"

"When I was a young boy."

"Go on."

"Well, when I was a young boy, a year was a long time. But then I grew older and the years, they didn't last nearly as long. Oh, this cruel trick of fate! As the years grew more important to me, the shorter and shorter they became! It was like trying to grasp each grain of sand as it fell through my hand!"

"Ah, but the years themselves didn't change, old man. They always contained the same amount of sand. It was your *perception* of them that changed."

"I understand, I understand, dear sir."

A pause, for the old man did not understand at all.

"Adventure, then. I haven't lived enough, dear sir!"

"Ah, but did I not give you the ability to do any sort of adventuring?"

"Well, not *exactly*—"

"Were you not born with two arms, two legs, a functioning brain?"

"Yes, yes I was."

"Then why did you not accomplish all of your adventuring?"

"It was my courage, sir! You simply didn't give me enough courage!"

"Ah, but courage is not something I can *give* you. It is something you must create within yourself."

"Oh, but please sir, may I have more time?"

"What do you need more time for?"

"For women, sir! Surely you can understand!"

"Oh, but why do you need more time for that?"

"Because I never got to have all the ones I wanted, dear sir! There are so many, and yet so little time for them all!"

"I could give you a thousand eternities and you would never sleep with all the women you desire."

"Well, I'd at least like to *try*—"

"No, old man, don't you see? The women are finite. It is your appetite for such desires that is infinite. Do you believe you could ever be satisfied with them all?"

"Yes, yes, a thousand times, *yes*!"

"It is not all the women in between that matter, old man, but the one at the end. You needed to find the one with which your soul harmonizes, for she will satisfy you more than all the rest whose hearts your anchors cannot catch."

"But...but....I don't *understand* you, dear sir. And *this* is why I need more time!"

"You need more time to understand?"

"Yes, dear sir, *yes!*"

"But there is nothing to understand, old man. Any man's understanding can be exchanged for another, and another, and another. You have demonstrated this with your requests..."

"I..."

"So what would you have *liked* more time for?"

"I..."

"Come now, even I cannot extend time forever."

"For my children, dear sir! And for my mama and papa too!"

"Why do you need more time for them?"

"I didn't spend my time with them when I was alive, dear sir!"

"What did you spend it on instead?"

"Adventuring, women, money—chasing *you* dear sir!"

"Ah, but I don't exist at all, old man. You're simply talking to yourself. And now there is no time left at all."

"No, wait...please, oh please, may I please have more time—?"

Part 2

The Best We Can Hope For
Or, Hall of Famer

The best we can hope for
Is that the drink does not kill us.
That our jobs do not defeat the fire
Needed to appreciate existence,
That we do not grow so embittered,
We blindly hate optimists,
And that our children put up with us,
Forgive us,
For this rotten planet we've left them.

Will it suffice to say,
That we made money as we destroyed it?

The best we can hope for,
Is to not be too frightened,
At the end,
The benefits of hardships and tragedies:
They break us,
Make us, ready to die,
We will not grasp for our forefathers gods,
As cowards do,
Spurred by the terror of regret,
Of minutes,
if only if only if only
Spent differently.

The best we can hope for,
Is to die a Hall of Famer,
The ghost's in our machines,
Carried slowly through a memory,
Of our moment of greatness,
When, for a thin sliver of existence,
We defeated the march of time,
And surpassed this ephemeral life,
To become a legend,
A master with skills so sharpened,
We redefined what it meant to be human,
A snapshot with confetti waiting,
Beads of sweat emerging,
The flash of photographs bursting,
Victory over a life where we can do nothing but lose in the
        end,
For a moment,
Achieved.

My Bachelor Year

I am disgusting,
Residing in a residual stew
Of sweat and grime,
Grease stains coat everything,
And I wallow in filth amidst
Piles of dirty clothes.

I haven't showered since last morning,
But why bother?
The porn stars don't mind,
Resolutely remaining the perfect mistress:
Perpetually willing, requiring nothing.

I smoke,
Roll over and play another episode,
Stretching myself in the sunlight like a cat,
I eye a half eaten pizza
Languishing on the coffee table.

I relish the lack of responsibilities,
But I do not want to die like this,
A cockroach,
Wallowing in the same childish life,
Of greasy food and getting fucked up,
Of sleeping till noon,
Of waking up just to jerk off,

I gorge myself,
Overdosing on hedonism and freedom,
Till the stench of it sickens me,

And I welcome the fate
Of booked Sundays to Bed Bath & Beyond.
I will steep myself in those moments,
Ignoring all those older men
Grasped by mid-life crises,
Who never learned to enjoy
The passing clouds of self,

For what is life,
But a series of identities?
Child, adolescent, young
Meandering adult,
To the married man, the retired man,
To the child again,
To the trees and dirt and dust,
To the stars and planets above,
To the atoms and elements,
To all that defines us,

We are only apes for a moment after all,
For all the rest of it,
We are...

Barriers

"There are no barriers,"
was the first truth Plant told me,
"You are an ape on Rock
falling through space.
All
Other
Things
are facets of your consciousness."

"You have nothing
to worry about."

"Your Self constructed and Self sustained
escapist insecurities,
are objects,
of a bored and spiritually sick consciousness.
You can simply turn away from them."

"Isn't enlightenment easy?"
Plant said, "All moments are beautiful,
and the ones to come,
Beautifully Unknown.
This paradise erupts with possibilities,
stifled only by
the apes who let old ideas drive,
the psychopaths who profit,
in status and trinkets,
by expanding the destruction
of your rock, your species,
of the other beings

that temporarily segregate
atoms into Individuality,
of all the different names you have for
Home."

"Here's how you hurt
the other people in your life,"
Plant said, "Don't become sad.
No one taught you how to be perfect,
and the journey of the ape
is to strive towards perfection,
not to be born with it.
So listen:
do you feel how you hurt them?"

I was all those I loved,
which was everyone.

"Tread kindly;
you have nothing to prove.
Don't you want to be better than those
who repress the things that shame them?"

I see myself from those I love,
Honesty boiling over,
Ego lashing out,
The ape misinterpreting
Disappointment as Anger,
Misapplying it in a tragic,
Unchangeable loop through the past,
Towards friends, family,
Lovers.

"Is that the type of ape
You want to be?"

The beautiful unknown beamed.

"There are no barriers,"
Plant said, "Human knowledge is a construct,
a satellite built of language
orbiting an ape's consciousness.
You are not separated from Ocean,
From Mountain,
From Grass and Atom,
Through time."

I Just Want To Fuck Something

Lesile's twenty two and swoons when I speak,
(Too young to see my sermons as bullshit),
But the problem is this:
She won't touch my dick.
Courtship strung across countless days,
And nothing but an angry erection
Rubbing against her abdomen,
Until I concede, strap on a latex sheath,
And perform my stand up routine of foreplay
Perfected across the Baltimore bars,

The biting of the neck,
Hot and cool breath across her chest,
Fingers slipping inside and around
Before meandering,
To the crest of her ass
And finally back,
My mouth massaging her lips,
Each lick increasing the angle of her arched back,
Until her hips muffle my ears
And I only hear my own slurps,
Swallows,
The slow burn of a tired tongue.

She finishes, condenses into a puddle
Upon the bed,
While I wipe my mouth on her sheets,

I
simply
am
The angry erection between us,
Still untouched.

Christ.

I live with two women,
Both of whom
Bring home a man the next night.
Between the walls I hear faint moans and
Lie, alone, erect,
Awake to empty wine glasses,
Ditzy, happy aloofness from them both,
"Oh, he's just so funny!"
I remain stewed in the musk of testosterone.

I am not a poet at this point.
Only an ape,
Venting frustration,

Stomping around till I make it to the gym,
Where I beat off frustration
On squats, deadlifts, chest,
Afterwards,
I take my dick in hand with determination,
Honestly afraid of the orgasm that awaits,
And when it comes I'm blinded,
Gone,
The ego obliterated,
I unleash gorilla loads into toilet paper,

The sparks of god flash with each pump
Until finally,
For a few heartbeats,
I am free of desire.

But the quarts of testosterone are biblical floods,
And the hand of god cannot build levees strong enough,
To stop the sheer stomp of horniness,

Sigh,
it is all pointless.

In a sweaty mess,
I still clench a mass of torn toilet paper,
Until,
The phone blips,
It's Leslie,

"Do you want to come over tonight?"

Mentally I lay out my case
For reciprocated foreplay,
Giving credence to the
Common conception that most men
Are bad at sex,
But insisting that women,
Aren't automatically,
Good at it.

But I say nothing,
Conceding that maybe
We're all bad in our own ways,

Prisoners of insecurities and nerves,
Blocking our ability to be comfortable,
And therefore,
To cum.

We speak of nothing,
Communication burned upon the bedpost,
Our continual sacrament to the puritan approach,
Distorting sex, ourselves,
And society,
Best indulge our trust and fetishes
To internet porn,
Where we cannot be rejected, or
Our flaws displayed,
Thus, vulnerability is an unknown state,
But then again,
So is,
Intimacy.

An Ethical Debate

A good American citizen,
My duty, to obediently consume
Products and opinions.
I am a man of contradictions,
I preemptively separate freedom with
An Arab girl's pink matter matted against a wall,
Her father, a fool,
Ungrateful for the liberty we give him,
He screams, he cries—
God, I'm so
fucking
bored.

Bring our boys home!
I'll sign the petition,
But not do too much more,
And only if the economy can withstand
Peace.
If not,
Fuck her father with the American phallus,
—The bomb—
His blood, or hers,
Will fuel our economy,
And this, another contradiction where I excel:
Deifying the unreal and blasphemizing the real.

In the land of opportunity
Cancer only affects the cells,
Of the lazy, the unemployed, the uninsured.

Like the meat stocks of our factory farms,
Suffering ignored or justified:
"We name these facts
Externalities,"
Or perhaps these beings made mistakes,
While the rich made mistakes extinct.

Patrick Bateman should have been named
Buddha.

We white wash these images,
Sitcom-ize our reality,
Hardships evaporate at the
Thirty minute mark,
And an ocean of irrational discourse
Suffocates us,
Bakes our psychosis in anxiety,
Until our national discourse is spewed
From the Ministry of Fox News:
Faggots fucking at 6,
Whores corrupting at 7,
A laugh track at 8,

You have no reason to be unhappy,
And yet, you are.
Well, that's your problem, and yours alone,
Even if,
In the confines of my home,
I feel it too.

We're not in this together,
There are no families or friends in America—
Only business contacts,
People to manipulate,
Or could manipulate you!
Constant vigilance annihilates trust,
And perfects our Insanity,

This, the last American achievement:
The mind of contradictions,
The mind of the superfluous,
The mind malleable to misconstruing morality,
Which wilts through the long winter
Of our post empire collapse.

The mind,
Like the intestines of a boy,
Dolloping the top of our final hor d'oeuvre:
The American War.

Dancers

My wandering hand unsnaps her bra,
"I just have to let you hear this song,"
She says,
As the tips of my fingers spark against
The soft curves of her chest.
She stands, the bra
Falling to the ground,
And starts dancing...

"I'm not doing this for you..."
She says,
And I believe her.
"I just like the way it makes me feel."
Sprawled back across her bed
I nod,
"Keep going,"
She pulls up her shirt, lets it fall,
The crest of her breast peeks out,
—Perfect little mounds—
Before she drops to an effortless split,
Yoga pants hugging her ass and
A reflexive erection arises.

"Come here."
I say,
But she just keeps dancing.
"I was with twenty guys by the time I was
Eighteen,"
She says, watching my face
For traces of surprise,

But finds nothing.
Looks down,
Smiling.

I don't tell her I lost my virginity
At eighteen.

When did I become addicted
To the absurd?
Maybe when I realized,
That only obedient lives are rewarded with success,
An army of automatons quelling philosophical dissent,
With a routine of cubicles and clinically prescribed
Opinions to preach,
And thoughts to think,
Bodies perishing with the most pleasant of
Smiles,
Believing,
They were free.

"I used to do heroin."
She says, turning her back to me.
"Why?"
"Because it was amazing, and
I didn't really have a reason,
Not to."
"Snort it or shot it?"
I ask, unfazed.
"Both."

She drops to another split,
And for the first time I notice
Two bruises,
Across her neck.

"How big is your dick?"
She asks.
"Five and a half or six inches,
Depending on the day,
Or how long its been since I've had
Sex."
"You were with Jen last night."
She's right.
"And you were with Alex."
She gets up,
Pouts her way to the bed,
"I don't want to dance anymore."

But still, she rests herself against me,
The spark between her thighs and mine
Beckoning,
I pull off her pants and panties
In a wad,
And she says,
"You won't want to talk to me
After I have sex with you."

This is true.
Her only value to me
Is getting off,
But I have no value to her.
We are simply,

Buoys adrift
In what our parents called Adulthood,
Tribeless wanderers,
Hoping only for the empathy of strangers.
We are children pretending,
To be adults, animals pretending,
To be humans, passengers pretending,
To be in control.

Her pussy is sprawling,
Unshaven,
Hair dots her thighs and pelvis,
"I won't get wet,"
She says,
"I can't get wet if I don't know the person."
"You know me," I lie,
And she shrugs, drunk,
Pulls my dick out
As if she really has nothing better
To do.

Suddenly reinvigorated,
She stands,
The song still dripping through weak speakers,
And with her shirt on, hair down,
She gets right up in front of my face,
Pulling her pussy lips back
In a wide grin of tender and dry skin,
And she says,
"See?
Nothing."

I Am Not The Man You Loved

Darling, did you know,
I never get over anything,
I just learn to live with it.
I bet everything on my old identity,
Which collapsed under the
Naïve beliefs of dreams
Forever unfulfilled.
And I'm not so sure
That I'll ever be the same,
Perhaps I am not meant to be.

But you said I was a good man.
Can I be him again?
You see, darling, I'm sick.
I spend the nights I'm alone
Looking for your ghost,
Because if I meet her again,
And she loves me again,
Will I be a good man
Again?

Darling, did you know,
I never let go of anything,
I just learn to live with it.
There's a secret that keeps me awake,
With shame I now admit,
To you,
The paper, the pen, my only lover,
I'm afraid I'll never get any better,

That I cannot any longer,
Acclimate myself to this culture.
I'm too diseased, too deranged,
For any good woman to love anymore.

You see, darling, I'm sick,
And I fully accept,
I am not the man you loved,
For I do not want to be him,
He was a boy, a child,
Arrogantly avoiding adulthood.
What I need to know, is:
Can I be a good man,
Again?

Repercussions

I drank too much,
Laid awake too late,
And smoked too much,
But it was worth it.
My attempt at living,

Tonight
I'll do it again.

Partaking in civilizations playgrounds,
Which replace the old prairie
Where my ancestors hunted,
My late night escapades
Scratch an evolutionary itch,
That progress has ironed out.

All of these other lives,
At youth, were ripe
With potential,
Possibly bending,
To a dissimilar shape
When stretched out,
Over the time span of a life.
Instead they hug the bends,
And encircle the bars,
And fellate the acceptable forms
Of conformity,

All these people,
Too afraid to fail,

To think,
Customizing their prison
To fulfill the illusion
That it was their choice,
To live,
Exactly like everyone else.

Sometimes when I'm feeling
Romantic, I'll daydream
Of taking a drive,
Leaving at midnight
And heading towards the ocean,
Alone.
It would beat drinking at a bar
Until two,
And prove I am different than all these
Identical people.

But instead I stay up too late,
Drink too much,
Smoke too much,
Never fuck enough,
Every humid night,
After humid night,
Grasping towards a life
I'd be proud to say I lived,
Rather than their hand me down,
From the worst generation,
That everyone else,
Seems okay
To lie in.

Twenty Something

Smoke billows off a cup of bitter coffee,
My stomach churns,
Attempting to digest
Whiskey, beer,
Thru an ocean of bile
Which kudzu's up my esophagus.
I taste it,
And drink the bitter coffee,
Gladly.

She entangled herself in my legs,
Giggling,
Persistence defeating indifference.
She's a "twenty something":
An adult in a dying empire,
A scavenger surviving,
On the scraps of success
The baby boomers left her.
A generation steeping
In their decade of immobility,
Yet plump with perpetual emotion,
That exists,
Yet remains unspoken.

The whiskey gives birth
To an ephemeral love,
A burst of creation
Causing hands to clasp,

And with her hair in my fist,
Moans and a thick mist paint the windows,
Amidst pierced breasts pressed against my lips,
Hips harmonize in desperate thrusts--
Until,
The passion crests.

Afterwards,
The bottle spins,
And one of us will feel boredom
The other, enrapture.

Which is my turn?

The Diner At The Edge Of The Universe

There's a diner at the edge of the universe,
An auxiliary entity lost,
In the forgotten darkness
Of capitalism,
Where the women are diner wrenches,
twenty year younger versions
of dead eyed, plump bellied, mascara scarred,
Waitresses of every town between
Barstow and Amarillo,
Vile crows feeding off
Coffee stained change,
While slowly hollowed out inside,
From fake smiles and subsisting off
Minimum wage.

The women are alleyway cats clawing at each other,
Echo's of which reverberate across the tables,
Shriveling up their tips.
They hiss and gossip over
A constantly refreshing series of injustices,
Greasy, black haired bastards,
Their conniving souls seeping out of their pores,
Marring whatever beauty
They may have been born with.

The women have all captured,
A neutered male
Who's too afraid to live on his own,
Preferring an imprisonment that's slow and safe,
When it's spread out over twenty years,

The sorrow of wasted potential
Dimming slowly,
Inside.

It's romantic to be poor in Portland in your twenties,
But unwanted babies will disperse these creatures,
To cities such as Barstow,
Amarillo,
Until a young man stumbles across them,
during his nomadic days
When he is still searching,
For something he believes can be found,

And he will wonder…
What were these women like,
In their twenties?
Were they sweet, pretty things?
Did the world slowly turn them
Into this mouth breathing stump of despair,
Crusted with defeat and swaddled
With the tumors of failure?

And he will think:
God,
I hope I don't ever become
That.

Myths to Live By

The Writer's Myth:
When these words fulfill ambition
and bring to fruition a greatness so vast,
Meaning is bestowed
In droplets of wisdom,
To the pallbearers of parched lips,
Thinkers, doubters,
Humans…
Thirsty and searching
For purpose,
Work so imbued with glory,
As to justify the atrocities
Of humans aping god.

Sobriety's listless slumber
Stumbles into epiphanies:
We lack the myths that engender meaning,
Myths that carried our consciousness across
The turbulent seas of survival,
Creating ironclad bounds of community.

Secularism severs spirituality,
Yet we still grasp for the ghost limbs of heritage,
Aging into elders still
Suckling upon the withered breasts
Of religion,
For watery platitudes of wisdom,
Too afraid to stick our toes
Into the ocean of the unknown…

We were never taught,
How to live without vices.
Our myths consist of
Enabling broken apes;
Alcoholics,
Gamblers, obese television
Bingers,
All encouraged by the vested interests
Of capitalism,

We are all orphans,
Unable to fathom the reasons
To withhold hedonistic religions–
Smoking, black tar coffee,
And seeping souls in moon shine whiskey,
We try to dull the pervasive migraines,
Of aimless lives inside
Hollow cultures,
Inside
An indifferent,
Universe.

Ricocheting from inflicting pain
Upon one stranger after another,
We stumble into ditches,
Celebrated in renaming ceremonies called
Marriages,
These lazy, culling comforts weather ourselves,
Against the elements
Of civilization–

Random accidents, diseases,
Debts and downsizes,
Recurring arguments against
Our ego's insistence of relevance.

We all live the same life,
Wanderers in the wreckage of
Inarticulate wants, desires, thoughts,
Billowing up from the great fog of
consciousness,
Forced to participate in a physical realm,
Where daily prayers of self-deceit
Are the social norm;
Cartoonish apes with elongated grins,
Pulled taut from the invisible pins of social pressure;
By all outward appearances,
We are all
So,
Happy, content,
All questions
Answered.

American Alcoholics

I drink to stop thinking.
Disquieting facts bubble up
To my frontal lobe,
Like:
Existence makes no inherent sense.
Why must life end?
Why do gargantuan holes
Of darkness suck up stars?
Why am I so frightened,
When I peek at the unfiltered
Preciousness of each moment?

Surely I should be doing something
More honorable than drinking;
Weren't gods such as humans
Made for grander lives?

This stool pools the alcohol drool
Across my consciousness,
Allowing me to forgo antagonizing truths
That sprout from the hours
Of totalitarian labor.
And so,
I am free,
From thoughts
I don't have the courage,
To confront.

Like,
There's only one affordable,
Available on every corner,
Medicine—the drink.
The rest are illegal,
Or sold in pill form for profit.
And,
The only help that exists
Is religion and the drink,
And the only fool more foolish
Than the drinker is the priest.

But a man cannot avoid forever,
That which always remains:
I am a cog unworthy of repair to my culture,
And what man wants to live
—or die—
like this?
Without honor,
With only what remains of regret,
And the desire for another drink.
For the blinds to be pulled over their eyes,
Ever harder, ever darker each night.

Take Me Back

Take me back,
time travel with me,
and we'll relive only the best pieces
of all my memories.
From the summer beach,
and to the bed I toast,
cheers to the sleepless nights,
and the weaving words we spoke.

And in the back of my mind,
I have to cry,
since those days,
have I felt truly alive?

I held in my hand,
a tender heart of 18,
and I squeezed it masochistically
just to see it bleed,
And I believe that we learn
from experiences like these,
That love seldom comes
as sweet as yours did to me.

Remains

What remains when old friends are gone?
Dispersed to different cities,
Malleable to the march of time,
The remnants of memories
Idle.

They cannot save you.
Life is a burden each man
Must carry on his own.
Above your grave they'll wait,
Drink to a man they knew,
Amiable company buys memories,
And someone to bury you.

What remains when girlfriends are gone?
There's no story to tell,
Anymore.
You're not a young man in love,
Or resting in the wreckage,
Of failed relations,
Even the yearnings of regret,
Are elusive.

They cannot save you.
So many marriages motivated
By someone achieving personal completion,
The misconception
That the struggle of who they are,
Ends.

Oh, what a tangible heaven.

What remains when the family is gone?
A buoy drifting through the sea of this country,
It's motion moved by kindness,
A sorrowfully understated
Trait of strangers,
Orphaned by fate,
And all of our apeish mistakes,
Eclipsing parenthood
As the standard purpose,
Of existence.

What remains when God is gone?
Nothing.
The question is a simultaneous
Revelation and eulogy,
It extinguishes meaning, resurrects doubt,
Annihilates the assumption
That our lives, our selves,
Are endowed with purpose.
Thankfully,
This realization lasts only a moment,
For the belief is resilient:
Nothing remains
When meaning leaves.

So we all march onward,
Ape's stomping through time,
Inflation infecting the worth of moments,
And civilization's cocaine ladened pace
Killing reflection,

We still believe in sense and purpose,
Making it blasphemous to admit,
That existence is just a psychedelic ride,
To which an ape's language is applied.

And so,
Fair well,
Bon voyage to another buoy.
I may never meet you,
But know that I love you.
And would kiss and hold and laugh with you,
Because you are as lost as us all.
And because you want so badly to be loved,
And to love,
And thus,
Suddenly,
Something remains.

Intimacy In Your Twenties

Her dress oozed voluptuousness,
And a velvety aura of obnoxious perfume,
Habitually drowning inhibition
In drinks, shots,
Broken exclamations barked
Into each other's ears,
Above a hollowed sense of normalcy.

The number of women a man has fucked
Are totems of achievement in his twenties.
They are,
Lacerated earlobes dangling around his neck,
Helping to craft an identity to deceive women:
"The most interesting man in the room for three hours."
But what type of man,
Awakes
In the morning sun?
Will he record the recitals of his children?
Prepare the estate,
Of a dying loved one?

We rename our hypocrisies
Complexities while we age,
The faces of our identity
Shifting,
As necessary,
So that our fetishes of survival
–Concessions in
Economic, social or relative lands–
Mutilate us just the same

As these one night stands,
Disfiguring our ability,
To see the worlds behind women's eyes,
That exist
Before and after,
We're gone.

The numbers rise with age,
And "love" becomes
Another conceit,
One where the jaded eye ebbs
Whatever once shined.
But the seasons of life still progress;
Cynicism decays, and
As wisdom blooms, a man
Comes to understand the depth of self and soul
Within him,
And her,
As empathy pollinates
Those smiles and curves,
He once ravaged with mindless lust,
Revealing the burgeoning seed of a new desire:
Can I trust her?

I remember the red dress and palms entrenched in ass,
Dirty words slurred over sweat,
"I want you to cum on my chest."
But also her standing
In my doorway, shivering,
"Can I sleep in your bed?"
And then a hesitant spooning,
The inching forward of affection between strangers,

Who've been more intimate
With each other,
Than with those who pretend
To know us so well.

And finally,
The nuzzle
Of her foot upon mine,
For warmth.

Sobriety
Or, My Roaring Twenties

I want to be drinking,
But instead,
I'm listening to an acoustic punk band playing,
Stripped down naked,
To the tender heart and simple truths I always heard
Above those thrashing chords,

I remember believing in
Something,
But the sensation remains unsalvageable,
And all that's left of hope
Are achievable dreams,
Like: a job,
Where my body is free to rot.
The slow creative fade,
Greased by something that breaks
Inside.

I want to be drinking,
But instead,
I'm thinking about how
We're not quite friends anymore,
These things ebb and flow,
Until something--
Ponderous nights alone with whiskey--
Shifts the mind of a man,
"Civilization expires friendship for the sake
Of old age, marriage or the economy,"

(Do you hear the dull roar of hollow rants?

…I do).

Or maybe,
There's no one to blame it on anymore,
Maybe we've simply failed each other.

I want to be drinking,
But instead,
I'm listening to music like I did,
When I was fifteen,

Alone.

And I dreamed a kaleidoscope dream
Of the dye's that would craft my life,
But now it's all whittled down,
To the drab, dull ache of
Lowered expectations,
Cheap whiskey, good friends, and enough money,
That I don't have to think about money
Too much.

Maybe I am just old and alone and all too aware,
Of how we're all dancing on a precipice of despair,
Pretending we've earned our place and fate respects
Arrogance.

But really we're only a mistake removed,
From the widow who
Routinely eats alone at the bar,
Or the homeless scabs asking
For money no one has,

These were once
Children,
Until
Life wore away hope,
Like wind smoothes slabs of rock.

I want to be drinking,
But instead,
I'm watching snow falling,
Three days sober.

Well,
I guess that's
Something.

Making Friends,

It's the mental equivalent of
Catching a cold:
Shame,
Induced by assumptions borne
Of loneliness.
But holding an undeniable mass,
As measured in the difference
Between what I assumed
Of our friendship,
And what you did not.

I have no justification,
For feeling betrayed--
We are not lovers,
Nor have we known each other,
Long,
And yet,
There it is.
A cloud depressing my
Consciousness,
For a day,
Or two,
Until I forget laughter,
Conversations of being older,
And the feeling of aspiring to something
We don't even want.

Surely I'm just too sensitive,
But this comes from such a persistent question,
Do I open the old wound,
Or bury it?

Strangers

In all the time in between
I recreated who I believed you to be,
An entity ceased,
When I see you
Before you even say it:
"Donovan."
I look up, feign surprise.
Did I order an awkward encounter,
With an ex with my coffee?
Apparently.

"What happened to San Diego?"
You gloat so well with just your eyes,
But the sinful smirk helps.
I should have worn a suit,
For its best to be well dressed,
When she's come to watch you burn.

Well,
At least I showered.

I ask nothing of her,
What is there to say?
There's a novel between us,
Of morning caresses,
Of smiles and kisses,
And the burning carcasses,
Of indigent love seeking revenge,
Oh, the miseries bequeathed when
Strangers love each other,

Because that's what we are, darling:
Strangers.
No matter what memories the ether
Holds in its heart.

The Shadows of Baltimore

Would you rather memories coat cities
In a yearning to return,
Or ricochet soundlessly against arteries,
As another bout of reminiscence
Is spurred by a name,
Photo,
A visitor
In the ether of your dreams...

I will remain where I am,
Until the shadows of heartbreak,
Come to infect
The nooks,
And scars of Portland,
As they did before,
When we were young fools,
Plucking tender secrets
From the confessions of friends,
And mashing them together until our edges ran smooth
And we felt nothing for each other,
The dust particles of affection spiraling outward,
Coating the architecture of Fells in
In a snowfall of sorrow and regret.

I see her coming
Like,
A comet through the ether of the future,
Careening into my atmosphere,
Where the molecules of our realities will intertwine,

And suddenly plentiful moments
Will spark against the divine,
In flashes of rapture we named
Love.

In my ancestral attempts
To place,
A plan upon chaos,
I promise to never make this mistake again,
But it's all inevitable.
Passion will drug reason
And in its slurred vision,
The infliction of revenge will seem
The most sensible option,
Bursting the comet above the ocean,
Where,
Months later,
As I ponder passing windows,
Alone,
Casting off rain and déjà vu,
The streaks will fall from the sky,
Smearing the conversations of bars,
The silence of book stores,
And the laughter of ocean shores,
With the oil spill pouring from the sky,
Spoiling the places that were once plump with hope,
And leaving nothing but the shadows
Of heartbreak,
And an idle wonder:

Would you rather remember a place fondly
Or never wish to return?

The Ghosts Of Kent State

News bubbles up
In the cells we spend our days,
"Inequality reaches new highs
Under—"
Another man bearing scarlet
CIA sponsored
Crosshairs,

How many times must we reelect the lesson
We are only our own saviors…

We follow,
The daily American slaughter,
Commutes and white collar labor
Replace ideals and beliefs,
With philosophical Styrofoam,
"Did you see the royal
Ba-by?"
Gleefully shirking social responsibility,
We leave the future in the ill-suited hands
Of Bohemians and capitalists,
Different responses to
Hopelessness.

At least there will be
An electronic record,
Of happy, deluded apes,
Dancing around the fire of
A decaying empire.

But reminders slip through
Our information tubes,
Spasms of fellow humans responding
Differently:
"Morsi ousted! Dozens of protesters,
Slaughtered!"
"Is it a coup?"
"Well," the talking head spins,
"Not *technically*."
Realpolitik jargon
For brain matter matted against a wall,

Egyptians know the power within their fists, within
Molotov cocktails and tear gas,
And they know
The repercussions,
Bullet holes obliterate beliefs of
Personal sovereignty,
And you still believe you're free?!

Do you remember
When we were young,
And we wrote protest songs?
Remember,
When outrage burst forth from
Belief
Made of hope,
Or some other tattoo
Of naivety.

So bring over the whiskey, friends,
And like all the men and women before,
Those that raised stones
Or words or swords,
For kings whose only dust remains,
We are the great innumerable masses,
Left to ruminate the sufferings we cannot change,
In bars and homes,
Lamenting the sunrise to come,
When everything
Will always
Be,
The same.

One Of Those Days
Or, The Sadness Is Infinite

The winter has made me lonely,
And you're the most comfortable thing around.
Cast off from overcast skies
I curl up in your company, idly wondering,
What is intimacy?

I kiss your back while we sway
In and out of sleep,
The waves of unconsciousness lapping at our brains,
Wet drags of lips across
The nape of your neck,
Reminders you are here,
Are real.

The morning comes and the slave chime beckons.
It's been ringing for so,
So long.

Trading existence for trinkets,
And food stamps,
Money is the global religion:
Puppet strings raising guns,
Amassing armies doe-eyed to the sight of death,
Yet enlivened with the power of god,
Overriding free will and controlling billions,
Innocent civilians become soldiers,
Shareholders, CEOs.

The sadness is infinite.

"One of those days,"
Where the soul is compressed
Into a dense tumor of pain,
Side effects of the day's enslavement,
Drowned in that first drink,
The echoes of which ripple outward,
Casting shadows of my fate—
When does one begin to kill oneself,
To make it through the day?

The winter is lonely,
And the sky a weeping grey.
Restless hands re-check the time until
I just sit, and watch sheet after
Sheet of rain.

Your bus must be late.

The Impossible Past
Or, East Coast Blues

The repressing shores of home burn
From the dry heat of time,
A cargo of accumulated memories
Billowing up in thick smog,
Blurring, shifting, lines of self...

I listened to the itch of philosophical friction,
Singing, "Settling down will always
Seem like death, until…"
Travels bestowed growth
But stole old friends,
And now, steeped in silence,
We drink,
To make it through these visits,
White knuckled consciousness strapped
To the speed of each passing moment.

Substance abuse swallows up
East coast blues,
A fanciful distraction for drunk synapsis,
But what happens when
The years keep accumulating?

Forty-five suddenly arrives
Upon a creaking ship,
Sobriety screaming
"Mutiny!" against
An arrogant ego torching years,
As if they were infinite.

The dregs of youth weep, seize the steering wheel,
Careening the ape upon the shore of regret,
Where a sober self ruminates upon
The virgin potential of youth,
Now, a ghost,
Appearing in clear waves
And crystallized sand,
Reflections upon
The window panes of old age,
Vaguely recollecting when
The future could be,
Anything.

Nursing stale beer amongst these
East coast blues,
I remember leaving those burning shores,
And drifting upon the nation of the northwest.

And I think of you,
As old friends bicker,
The echoes of screams crashing through walls,
I am alone in the places I once called home,
And dream of the comfort, the arms,
Upon another coast,
The lighthouse of belonging,
Calling me home.

Thrash

Expunged from the womb of creation,
We grasp for love,
Our bloody hands and fertile minds
Exploding into confused cries.
A trillion neurons reaching out into this realm,
Smashed against the palm of archaic ideologies,
Of hatred and neuroses,
The permanent imprint of our fathers forgotten fates,
Ignorant men borne of an indifferent
Universe,
Grasping for meaning in animal religions.

They were not yet gods,
Not like us.

We thrash against our fathers' traditions,
An all-knowing ignorance guiding our paths,
Until the tumbling avalanche of adulthood
Humbles.
The weakness of these darkest nights,
Leaves us grasping for our mothers' wombs,
Our fathers' palms,
Oh, when they were gods.

We thrash against
The imprisoning bars of history,
Which extend in all directions,
Encompassing

All information,
Until it's distilled into an invisible, yet efficient
Prison.

Youthful rebellion ebbs into wisdom,
Defeated, it becomes
Lessons for the next generation,
Until it is lost in allegiances to conservative traditions,
Burying wisdom among the bones of our ancestors,
And across these naked philosophical prairies
Only arrogance remains,
Reinvigorated,
Encouraging man to continue being so
Civilized.

We thrash against the present,
The unknown moment that always arrives,
Through distractions or drinking,
Grasping for plans to place upon chaos,
And consistently distressed
When a seventy year long psychedelic trip,
Fails to conform to the linguistic confines,
Our feeble ape brain
Places upon it.

We thrash against our fragile ego's
Obsessing over how we're perceived,
Grasping, instead, for
Who we wish ourselves to be,
Hesitant to acknowledge this permanent difference,
In which lies our actual selves,
Encased securely in protective facades,

Grasping, instead, for the lies of becoming
Perfect,
Never awkward, without flaws,
Never vulnerable, always strong,
A mannequin embodying
Our culture's thin identity spectrum,
Nothing felt that the sitcoms do not subscribe,
Nothing said that the advertisements do not imply,
Our opinions plucked from their sterile sermons,
Our mannerisms determined from their gender
Compression,

Millions of twenty something children,
Thrashing against old institutions,
Grasping for the meaningful labor of salvation,
But waking, always, as slaves
To a world they were given,
Each morning, birthed into a horrific dimension,
Where atrocities are inflicted upon all living things,

At the behest of zealous Elders,
Who thrash against the wave of encroaching irrelevancy,
Grasping for control, madmen
Cackling over poisoned rivers,
Snorting thick lines of ideology off
The bloated bellies of African babies,
Screaming,
"WE KNOW WHAT'S BEST."

While stoic mountains and sick skies mourn
The sorrow sowed when apes deify opposable
Thumbs.

Released to the crashing waves of time,
We thrash against the shores of fate,
Grasping for elusive rocks of wisdom,
Find only decaying husks of religion
We grasp for the knowledge of old fathers,
Find nothing but absent devils,
We grasp for the love of old Mothers,
Find nothing but pillaged altars.
We grasp for love,
And find a semblance of
It in the musky den of our bedrooms,
Over the steam of coffee as sunlight spills
Across a hardwood floor,
Grasping for warm love and hope
And thrashing,
No more.

Available from Curious Apes Publishing:

The Evolution of Strangers
By Jonathon S. Kendall

Hello, World
By Steven Parton